jokes for blokes

Girl trouble

Spoilt for choice

A man is dating three women and doesn't know which one to marry. He decides to give them a test. He gives a present of

£3000 to each woman to see how they will spend it.

The first woman goes for a total make-over. She books into a smart beauty salon, gets her hair done, new make-up and buys several new outfits. Then she dresses up very nicely for the man. She tells him that she has done this to be more attractive for him because she loves him so much.

The man is impressed.

The second woman goes shopping to buy the man gifts. She gets him a new set of golf clubs, some new gizmos for his computer, and some expensive clothes. As she presents these gifts, she tells him that she has spent all the money on him because she loves him so much.

Again, the man is impressed.

The third woman invests the money in the stock market. She earns several times the £3000. She gives him back his £3000 and reinvests the remainder in a joint account. She tells him that she wants to save for their future because she loves him so much.

Obviously, the man is impressed.

The man thinks for a long time about what each woman has done with the money, and then he decides to marry the one with the largest breasts.

Great inventions

Arthur Davidson, founder of the Harley Davidson Motorcycle Corporation, died and went to Heaven. At the pearly gates, St Peter told Arthur, 'Since you've been such a good man and your motorcycles have changed the world, your reward is that you can hang out with anyone you want to in Heaven.'

Arthur thought about this for a minute and then said, 'I want to hang out with God.'

St Peter took Arthur to the Throne Room, and introduced him to God.

Arthur then asked God, 'Hey, aren't you the inventor of women?'

'Ah, yes,' answered God.

'Well,' said Arthur, 'professional to professional, you have some major design flaws in your invention. I'll tell you about them, if that's OK.

1. There's too much inconsistency in the front-end protrusion.
2. It chatters constantly at high speeds.
3. Most of the rear ends are too soft and wobble too much.
4. The intake is placed way too close to the exhaust.
5. The maintenance costs are outrageous.'

'Hmmmm, you may have some good points there,' replied God. 'Hold on.'

God went over to his celestial supercomputer, typed in a few words and waited for the results. The computer printed out a slip of paper, and God read it to himself.

'Well, it may be true that my invention is flawed,' God said to Arthur, 'but according to these figures, more men are riding mine than yours ...'

In touch with our feminine side

Leading scientists from Cambridge University recently reported that the results of an analysis revealed the presence of female hormones in beer, and suggested that men should take a look at their beer consumption.

The theory is that drinking beer makes men turn into women. To test the theory, 100 men were each given six pints of beer to drink within a one-hour period.

It was then observed that 100% of the men gained weight, talked excessively without making sense, became overly emotional, couldn't drive, failed to think rationally, argued over nothing, had to sit down while urinating and refused to apologise when wrong. No further testing is planned.

A credit card ad for men

Cover charge: £15.00

Round of drinks: £23.00

Lap dance: £30.00

Another round of drinks: £23.00

Another lap dance and tips: £50.00

A round of shots: £34.00

Private dance in your hotel room: £300.00

Send her on her way and never have to hear her complain: priceless

There are some things that money can't buy. For everything else, there's MisterCard.

Face facts

A woman was very distraught at the fact that she had not had a date in quite a long time. Afraid she might have something wrong with her, she decided to employ the medical expertise of a sex therapist. Her personal physician recommended Dr Wang, a well-known Chinese doctor working in that field.

So she went and saw him. On entering the examination room, Dr Wang took one look at her and said, 'Okay, take off aw your crows.'

She quickly disrobed and stood naked before him.

'Now,' said Wang, 'get dow on knees and craw reery, reery, fass away from me to the other side of room.'

When she had done as she was told, Dr Wang said, 'Okay, now turn around and craw reery, reery fass to me.'

Once again she obliged. Dr Wang slowly shook his head, 'Okay, your probrem vaywe, vaywe bad. You have Ed Zachary disease ... worse case I ever see ... that why you not have dates.'

Confused, the woman asked, 'What is Ed Zachary disease?'

Wang replied, 'It when your face rook Ed Zachary rike your arse.'

A fair cop

An elderly couple were travelling by car across the country. The woman was driving when she got pulled over by a traffic policeman. The officer said, 'Excuse me, madam, did you know you were speeding?'

The woman turned to her husband and asked, 'What did he say?'

The old man yelled, 'He says you were speeding!'

The policeman said, 'May I see your licence?'

The woman turned to her husband again and asked, 'What did he say?'

The old man yelled, 'He wants to see your licence!'

The woman handed the policeman her driving licence.

The policeman said, 'I see you are from Birmingham. I spent some time there once and had the worst sex I have ever had.'

The woman turned to her husband and asked, 'What did he say?'

The old man yelled, 'He says he thinks he knows you!'

Skin deep

Luke's wife bought a new line of expensive cosmetics, guaranteed to make her look years younger.

After a lengthy period sitting in front of the mirror applying the 'miracle' products, she asked, 'Darling, honestly, what age would you say I am?'

Looking her carefully up and down, Luke replied, 'Judging from your skin, 20; your hair, 18; and your figure, 25.'

'Oh, you flatterer!' she gushed.

'Hey, wait a minute!' Luke interrupted. 'I haven't added them up yet.'

How to be politically correct about women

She is not a BLEACHED BLONDE –

she is PEROXIDE DEPENDANT.

She is not a BAD COOK –

she is MICROWAVE COMPATIBLE.

She does not wear TOO MUCH JEWELLERY –

she is METALLICALLY OVERBURDENED.

She is not CONCEITED –

she is INTIMATELY AWARE OF HER BEST QUALITIES.

She does not GAIN WEIGHT –

she is a METABOLIC UNDERACHIEVER.

She does not TEASE or FLIRT –

she engages in ARTIFICIAL STIMULATION.

She is not TOO SKINNY –

> she is SKELETALLY PROMINENT.

She does not HAVE A MOUSTACHE –

> she is IN TOUCH WITH HER
> MASCULINE SIDE.

She does not HATE TELEVISED SPORTS –

> she is ATHLETICALLY BYPASSED.

She has not BEEN AROUND –

> she is a PREVIOUSLY ENJOYED
> COMPANION.

She does not WEAR TOO MUCH
PERFUME –

> she commits FRAGRANCE ABUSE.

She is not an AIRHEAD –

> she is REALITY IMPAIRED.

She does not get DRUNK or TIPSY –

she gets CHEMICALLY
INCONVENIENCED.

She does not get FAT or CHUBBY –

she achieves MAXIMUM DENSITY.

She is not COLD or FRIGID –

she is THERMALLY INACCESSIBLE.

She does not WEAR TOO MUCH
MAKE-UP –

she has reached COSMETIC
SATURATION.

She does not NAG YOU –

she becomes VERBALLY REPETITIVE.

Never too old to learn

Eight-year-old Sally brought her report card home from school. Her marks were good: mostly As and a couple of Bs. However, her teacher had written across the bottom of the report:

'Sally is a clever little girl, but she has one fault: she talks too much in school. I have an idea I am going to try, which I think may break her of the habit.'

Sally's dad signed her report card, putting a note on the back:

'If your idea works on Sally please let me know what it is, as I would like to try it out on her mother.'

(Nearly) always watching over you ...

A man was walking along the street when he heard a voice call out: 'Stop! Stand still! If you take one more step, a brick will fall down on your head and kill you.' The man stopped and, sure enough, a big brick fell to the floor right in front of him. The man was astonished.

He went on and, after a while, he was about to cross the road when, once again, the voice shouted out: 'Stop! Stand still! If you take one more step a car will run over you and you will die.' Again, the man did as he was instructed, just as a car came careering around the corner, barely missing him.

'Where are you?' the man asked. 'Who are you?'

'I am your guardian angel,' the voice answered.

'Oh yeah?' the man asked. 'So where the hell were you when I got married?'

It's the thought that counts

A lawyer, an accountant and a biker were having a drink together in a pub.

The lawyer suddenly said: 'It's our anniversary next week and I've bought my wife a diamond ring and a new car.'

The others said: 'Why have you bought her two presents?'

The lawyer said: 'Well, I thought that if she didn't like the ring, she would like the car and know that I love her.'

The accountant, not to be outdone, said, 'On our anniversary I bought my wife a 22-carat gold necklace and a two-week holiday in the Bahamas.'

The others said: 'Why did you do that?'

The accountant said: 'Well, I thought that if she didn't like the necklace, she would like the holiday, and know that I love her.'

The biker said: 'I bought my common-law wife a T-shirt and a dildo.'

The others said: 'Why did you do that?'

The biker said: 'Well, I thought that if she didn't like the T-shirt, she could go and f*** herself.'

Why don't they understand us?

Rules for women

1   Learn to work the toilet seat. You're
    a big girl. If it's up, put it down. We
    need it up; you need it down. You don't

hear us complaining about you leaving
it down.

2   Birthdays, Valentine's days and
anniversaries are not quests to see if
we can find the perfect present yet
again!

3   Sometimes we are not thinking about
you. Live with it.

4   Saturday = football. It's like the full
moon or the changing of the tides.
Let it be.

5   Don't cut your hair. Ever. Long hair is
always more attractive than short hair.
One of the big reasons blokes fear
getting married is that married women
always cut their hair, and by then
we're stuck with them.

6   Shopping is NOT a sport. And, no, we
are never going to think of it that way.
Ask for what you want. Let us be clear

on this one: subtle hints do not work! Strong hints do not work! Obvious hints do not work! Just say it!

7   We don't remember dates. Mark birthdays and anniversaries on the calendar. Remind us frequently beforehand.

8   Most blokes own three pairs of shoes and three tops. What makes you think we'd be any good at choosing which pair of your shoes, out of 30, would look good with your dress?

9   'Yes' and 'No' are perfectly acceptable answers to almost every question.

10   Come to us with a problem only if you want help solving it. That's what we do. Sympathy is what your girlfriends are for.

11   A headache that lasts for 17 months is a problem. See a doctor.

12   Check your oil! Please.

13 Anything we said six months ago is inadmissible in an argument. In fact, all comments become null and void after seven days.

14 If you won't dress like a lingerie advertisment, don't expect us to act like blokes from soap operas.

15 If you think you're fat, you probably are. Don't ask us. We refuse to answer.

16 If something we said can be interpreted two ways, and one of the ways makes you sad or angry, we meant the other one!

17 Let us ogle. We are going to look anyway; it's genetic.

18 You can either ask us to do something or tell us how you want it done. Not both. If you already know best how to do it, just do it yourself.

19 Whenever possible, please say whatever you have to say during commercials.

20 Christopher Columbus did not need directions, and neither do we.

21 ALL men see in only 16 colours, like computer default settings. Peach, for example, is a fruit, not a colour. Apple is also a fruit. We have no idea what mauve is.

22 If it itches, it will be scratched. We do that.

23 We are not mind-readers and we never will be. Our lack of mind-reading ability is not proof of how little we care about you.

24 If we ask what is wrong and you say 'nothing', we will act like nothing's wrong. We know you are lying, but it's just not worth the hassle.

25 If you ask a question you don't want an answer to, expect an answer you don't want to hear.

26 When we have to go somewhere, absolutely anything you wear is fine. Really.

27 Don't ask us what we're thinking about unless you are prepared to discuss such topics as belly-button fluff, the offside rule or subwoofers.

28 You have enough clothes.

29 You have too many shoes.

30 Foreign films are best left to foreigners (unless they star Bruce Lee or are some war flick where it doesn't really matter what the hell anyone's saying anyway).

31 It is neither in your best interests nor ours to fill out the questionnaire together. No, it doesn't matter which questionnaire.

32 Beer is as exciting for us as handbags are for you.

Thank you for reading this. Yes, I know, I have to sleep on the couch tonight, but didn't you know that we really don't mind that? It's like camping.

The ugly stick

The top 10 rejection lines given by men:
(and what they actually mean ...)

1   I think of you as a sister:
You're ugly.

2   There's a slight difference in our ages:
You're ugly.

3   I'm not attracted to you in 'that' way:
You're ugly

4   My life is too complicated right now:
You're ugly.

5   I've got a girlfriend:
You're ugly.

6   I don't date women where I work:
You're ugly.

7   It's not you, it's me:
You're ugly.

8 I'm concentrating on my career:

You're ugly.

9 I'm celibate:

You're ugly.

... and the all time favourite rejection line given by men:

10 Let's be friends:

You're the ugliest f***ing bitch that has ever existed on this planet.

The female of the species

No means p*ss off!

The top 10 rejection lines given by women
(and what they actually mean ...)

1 I think of you as a brother:

You remind me of that inbred banjo-
playing geek in *Deliverance*.

2 there's a slight difference in our ages:

You are one Jurassic geezer.

3 I'm not attracted to you in 'that' way:

You are the ugliest dork I've ever laid eyes upon.

4 my life is too complicated right now:

I don't want you spending the whole night or else you may hear phone calls from all the other blokes I'm seeing.

5 I've got a boyfriend:

… who's really my male cat and a large tub of chocolate ice cream.

6 I don't date men where I work:

I wouldn't even date you if you were in the same 'solar system' much less the same building.

7 It's not you, it's me:

It's not me, it's you.

8   I'm concentrating on my career:

Even something as boring and unfulfilling as my job is better than dating you.

9   I'm celibate:

I've sworn off only the men like you.

… and the all time favourite rejection line given by women:

10   let's be friends:

I want you to stay around so I can tell you in excruciating detail about all the other men I meet and have sex with to get the male perspective.

Womanspeak

1   I'm sorry = You'll be sorry.

2   We need = I want.

3   It's your decision = The correct decision should be obvious by now.

4   Do what you want = You'll pay for this later.

5   We need to talk = I need to complain.

6   Sure go ahead = I don't want you to do that.

7   I'm not upset = Of course I'm upset, you moron!

8   You're so manly = You need a shave and you sweat a lot.

9   Be romantic, turn out the lights = I have flabby thighs.

10 This kitchen is so inconvenient = I want a new house.

11 I want new curtains = and carpeting, and furniture, and wallpaper.

12 Hang the picture there = NO, I mean hang it there!

13 I heard a noise = I noticed you were almost asleep.

14 Do you love me? = I'm going to ask for something expensive.

15 How much do you love me? = I did something today you're really not going to like.

16 I'll be ready in a minute = Kick off your shoes and find a good football match on TV.

17 Does my bum look big in this? = Tell me I'm beautiful.

18 You have to learn to communicate = Just agree with me.

19 Are you listening to me?! = Too late, you're dead.

20 Was that the baby? = Why don't you get out of bed and rock him until he goes to sleep?

21 I'm not yelling! = Yes, I am yelling because I think this is important.

22 The same old thing = Nothing.

23 Nothing = Everything.

24 Everything = My PMT is acting up.

25 Nothing, really = It's just that you're such an idiot.

The hormone minefield

The hormone hostage knows that there
are days in the month when all a man has
to do is open his mouth and he takes his
life in his own hands.

So, cut out and keep the following handy
guidelines on how to say the right things
at this difficult time. Such a pocket guide
should be as common as a driving licence:
found in the wallet of every husband,
boyfriend or significant other.

DANGEROUS: What's for dinner?

SAFER: Can I help you with dinner?

SAFEST: Where would you like to go for
dinner?

ULTRASAFE: Have some chocolate.

DANGEROUS: Are you wearing that?

SAFER: Wow, you look good in brown.

SAFEST: WOW! Look at you!

ULTRASAFE: Have some chocolate.

DANGEROUS: What are you so worked up about?

SAFER: Could we be overreacting?

SAFEST: Here's 50 quid.

ULTRASAFE: Have some chocolate.

DANGEROUS: Should you be eating that?

SAFER: You know, there are a lot of apples left.

SAFEST: Can I get you a glass of wine with that?

ULTRASAFE: Have some chocolate.

DANGEROUS: What did you do all day?

SAFER: I hope you didn't overdo it today.

SAFEST: I've always loved you in that dressing gown!

ULTRASAFE: Have some more chocolate.

Boozy babes

Seven landlords were asked if they could identify a woman's personality on the basis of what drink she chose. Though interviewed separately, they agreed on almost all counts. The results were as follows.

beer

Personality: casual, low maintenance, down-to-earth

Approach: challenge her to a game of pool

cocktails with umbrellas

Personality: neurotic, a pain in the arse

Approach: avoid her, unless you want to be her cabin boy

cocktails, no umbrellas

Personality: mature, has picky taste, knows what she wants

Approach: if she wants you, she'll buy YOU a drink

wine (bottled not in a four-litre box)

Personality: conservative and classy, sophisticated

Approach: try to weave Paris and clothing into the conversation

alcopops

Personality: easy, thinks she is trendy and sophisticated, actually doesn't have a clue

Approach: make her feel smarter than she is and you're in

coffee liqueur

Personality: annoying voice, bit of a tart

Approach: stand close and mention the alley next to the pub

shorts (vodka, gin, etc.)

Personality: hanging out with male pals or looking to get drunk ... and naked

Approach: easiest hit in the pub, nothing to do but wait

Things you should never say to a woman during an argument

1 Don't you have some washing to do or something?

2 Ohh, you're so cute when you get all p*ssed off.

3 You're just upset because you're arse is beginning to spread.

4 Wait a minute – I get it. What time of the month is it?

5 Whoa, time out. The football's on.

6 Looks like someone had an extra bowl of bitchflakes this morning!

7 Is there any way we can do this via e-mail?

8 Who are you kidding? We both know that thing ain't loaded.

Four questions feared by men

1 What are you thinking about?

2 Do you love me?

3 Do I look fat?

4 Do you think she is prettier than me?

What makes these questions so difficult is that each one is guaranteed to explode into a major argument if the man answers incorrectly (i.e. tells the truth). Therefore, as a public service, each question is analysed below, along with possible responses.

question 1: what are you thinking about?

The proper answer to this, of course, is: 'I'm sorry if I've been pensive, dear. I was just reflecting on what a warm, wonderful, thoughtful, caring, intelligent woman you are, and how lucky I am to have met you.'

This response obviously bears no resemblance to the true answer, which most likely is one of the following.

a) Football.

b) Nothing.

c) How fat you are.

d) How much prettier she is than you.

e) How I would spend the insurance money if you died.

question 2: do you love me?

The proper response is: 'YES!' or, if you feel a more detailed answer is in order, 'Yes, dear.'

Inappropriate responses include the following.

a) Oh yeah, sh*t-loads.

b) Would it make you feel better if I said 'yes'?

c) That depends on what you mean by love.

d) Does it matter?

e) Who, me?

question 3: do I look fat?

The correct answer is an emphatic 'Of course not!'

Among the incorrect answers are the following.

a) Compared to what?

b) I wouldn't call you fat, but you're not exactly thin.

c) A little extra weight looks good on you.

d) I've seen fatter.

e) Could you repeat the question? I was just thinking about how I would spend the insurance money if you died.

question 4: do you think she's prettier than me?

Once again, the proper response is an emphatic 'Of course not!'

Incorrect responses include the following.

a) Yes, but you have a better personality.

b) Not prettier, but definitely thinner.

c) Not as pretty as you when you were her age.

d) Define 'pretty'.

e) Could you repeat the question? I was just thinking about how I would spend the insurance money if you died.

The ball and chain

What they say about marriage

Marriage is not a word. It's a sentence –
a life sentence.

Marriage is very much like a violin; after the sweet music is over, the strings are attached.

A marriage certificate is just another way of saying 'work permit'.

It's true that all men are born free and equal, but some of them get married!

A happy marriage is a matter of giving and taking; the husband gives and the wife takes.

There was once a man who said, 'I never knew what happiness was until I got married ... and then it was too late!'

They say that when a man holds a woman's hand before marriage, it is love; when he holds her hand after marriage, it's self-defence.

Always talk to your wife while you're making love ... if there's a phone handy.

Don't marry for money; you can borrow it cheaper.

If your wife wants to learn how to drive, don't stand in her way.

In marriage, as in war, it is permitted to take every advantage of the enemy.

Love thy neighbour, but make sure her husband is away first.

Marriage is the process of finding out what kind of man your wife would have preferred.

Fair exchange

A salesman is driving towards home in Croydon when he sees a hitchhiker thumbing a lift at the side of the road. Because the trip has been long and quiet, he stops the car to let the hitchhiker get in. After a bit of small talk, the hitchhiker notices a brown bag on the back seat.

'What's in the bag?' he asks the salesman.

'It's a bottle of wine. I got it for my wife,' he replies.

The hitchhiker is silent for a moment and then says, 'Good swap.'

Coffin dodger

A funeral service is being held for a woman who has just passed away. At the end of the service, the pallbearers are carrying the coffin out of the church when they accidentally bump into a wall, jarring the coffin. They hear a faint moan. Taking the lid off the coffin, they find that the woman is still alive!

She lives for ten more years and then dies. Another ceremony is held and, at the end of the service, the pallbearers carry out the coffin as before. As they are making their way out of the church, the husband shouts, 'Watch out for that wall!'

A load of bull

A man takes his wife to a stock show and they start heading down the alley where the bulls are tethered …

They come up to the first bull and, beside him, a sign states: 'This bull mated 50 times last year.' The wife turns to her husband and says, 'He mated 50 times in a year, you could learn from him.'

They proceed to the next bull and his sign states: 'This bull mated 65 times last year.' The wife turns to her husband and says, 'This one mated 65 times last year. That's over five times a month. You could learn from this one too.'

They proceed to the last bull and his sign says: 'This bull mated 365 times last year.' The wife's mouth drops open and she says, 'WOW! He mated 365 times last year. That's ONCE A DAY!!! You could really learn from this one.'

The man turns to his wife and says, 'Go and find out if it was 365 times with the same cow!'

The late escapee

A convicted felon was given ten years without parole for his latest crime. After two years in jail, he managed to escape. His escape was the lead item on the six o'clock news.

Obviously, he had to be careful not to be spotted, so he worked his way home on little-travelled routes, running across deserted fields and taking every precaution he could think of.

Eventually, he arrived at his house and rang the doorbell. His wife opened the door and bellowed at him, 'You good-for-nothing b*****d! Where the hell have you been? You escaped over six hours ago.'

A crying shame

A woman awoke during the night to find that her husband was not in bed.

She put on her dressing gown and went downstairs to look for him.

He was sitting at the kitchen table with a cup of coffee in front of him and a box of tissues. He appeared to be deep in thought, just staring at the wall.

When she got closer, she saw him wipe a tear from his eye before taking a tissue, blowing his nose and taking a sip of his coffee.

'What's the matter dear? Why are you down here at this time of night?' she asked.

'Do you remember 20 years ago when we were dating, and you were only 16?' he asked.

'Yes, I do,' she replied.

'Do you remember when your father caught us in the back seat of my car making love?'

'Yes, I remember.'

'Do you remember when he shoved that shotgun in my face and said, 'Either you marry my daughter, or spend the next 20 years in jail?'

'Yes, I do,' she said.

He wiped another tear from his cheek and said, 'You know ... I would have got out today.'

Two lovely black eyes

A man staggered into casualty with two black eyes and a golf club wrapped tightly around his throat. Naturally, the doctor on duty asked him what happened.

'Well, it was like this,' said the man. 'I was having a quiet round of golf with my wife when she sliced her ball into a field of cows. We went to look for it and while I was rooting around, I noticed one of the cows had something white poking out of its rear end. I walked over and lifted up its tail and, sure enough, there was my wife's golf ball ... stuck right in the middle of the cow's bum. That's when I made my mistake.'

'What did you do?' asked the doctor.

'Well, I lifted the tail and yelled to my wife, 'Hey, this looks like yours!''

What men expect in a wife

1 She will always be beautiful and cheerful.

2 She could marry a movie star, but wants only you.

3 She will have hair that never needs curlers or trips to the salon.

4 Her beauty won't run in a rainstorm.

5 She will never be sick – just allergic to jewellery and designer clothes.

6 She will insist on moving the furniture by herself – it's good for her figure.

7 She will be an expert in cooking, cleaning the house, fixing the car and the TV, painting the house, and keeping quiet.

8 Her favourite hobbies will be mowing the lawn and shovelling snow.

9 She will hate credit cards.

10 Her favourite expression will be, 'What can I do for you, dear?'

11 She will think you have Einstein's brain but look like Mr Universe.

12 She will wish you would go out with the boys so that she could get some sewing done.

13 She will love you because you're so sexy.

What men get in a wife

1 She speaks 140 words a minute, with gusts up to 180.

2 She was once a model for a totem pole.

3 Where there's smoke, there she is – cooking.

4 She's a light eater ... once it gets light, she starts eating.

5 She lets you know you have only two faults: everything you do and everything you say.

6 No matter what she does with it, her hair looks like an explosion in a steel wool factory.

7 If you get lost, open your wallet and she'll find you.

Through bad times ... and worse

A devoted wife was taking care of her husband, who had been slipping in and out of a coma for several months.

In a moment of clarity, he motioned for her to come near. 'You have been with me through all the bad times,' he said. 'When I got fired, you were there. When my business failed, you were there. When I got shot, you stayed by my side. When we lost the house, you gave me support. When my health started failing, you were still by my side. You know what?'

'What dear?' she asked gently.

'I think you bring me bad luck.'

Isle be seeing you ...

While enjoying an early-morning breakfast in a Cornwall cafe, three elderly men were discussing everything from football and fishing to the weather, and how things used to be in the 'good old days'.

Eventually, the conversation moved on to their spouses. One man turned to the chap on his right and asked, 'John, aren't you and your wife celebrating your 50th wedding anniversary soon?'

'Yes, that's right,' John replied.

'Well, are you going to do anything special to celebrate?' the other friend asked.

The old man pondered this for a moment, then replied, 'For our 25th anniversary, I took Betty to the Isle of Skye. Maybe for our 50th, I'll go up there and get her.'

In sickness and in health

A dietician was addressing a large audience in Newcastle: 'The material we put into our stomachs is enough to have killed most of us sitting here years ago. Red meat is awful. Soft drinks corrode your stomach lining. Chinese food is loaded with monosodium glutamate.

Vegetables can be disastrous, and none of us realises the long-term harm caused by the bacteria in our drinking water. But there is one thing that is the most dangerous of all and we have all eaten or will eat it.

Can anyone here tell me what food it is that causes the most grief and suffering for years after eating it?'

A 75-year-old man in the front row stood up and said, 'Wedding cake.'

Playing away

A bad business

A man walks into a nightclub, goes up to the bar and asks for a beer.

'Certainly, sir. That'll be one pence.'

'One pence?!' exclaims the man.

'Yes,' replies the barman.

The man then glances over at the menu and asks, 'Could I have a nice juicy T-bone steak, with chips, peas and a fried egg?'

'Certainly, sir,' replies the barman, 'but that comes to real money.'

'How much money?' the man enquires.

'Four pence,' the barman replies.

'Four pence? Where's the bloke who owns this place?' says the man, looking completely astounded.

'He's upstairs with my wife,' the barman replies.

'What's he doing upstairs with your wife?' asks the man.

'The same thing as I'm doing to his business,' retorts the barman.

Unlucky bet

This geezer is sitting reading his newspaper when his wife sneaks up behind him and whacks him on the head with a frying pan.

'What was that for?' he says.

'That was for the piece of paper in your trouser pocket with the name Thelma written on it,' she replies.

'Don't be daft,' he explains, 'two weeks ago when I went to the races, Thelma was the name of one of the horses I bet on.'

She seems satisfied at this, and goes off to do some housework. Three days later he's sitting in his chair reading when she hits him with an even bigger frying pan, knocking him out cold. When he comes round he says, 'What the hell was that for?'

'Your f***ing horse phoned!'

A hole in one?

A married man was having an affair with his secretary. One day, their passions overcame them and they took off for her house where they made mad passionate love all afternoon. Exhausted from the wild sex, they fell asleep, waking up at around 8pm.

As the man threw on his clothes, he asked the woman to take his shoes outside and rub them through the grass and dirt. Mystified, she nonetheless complied. He then slipped into his shoes and drove home.

'Where have you been?' demanded his wife when he entered the house.

'Darling, I can't lie to you. I've been having an affair with my secretary and we've been having wild sex all afternoon. I fell asleep and didn't wake up until eight o'clock.'

The wife glanced down at his shoes and said, 'You lying b*****d! You've been playing golf again!'

What a picture!

A man was paying his lawyer a visit. The lawyer said, 'I have bad news and worse news for you. Which would you like to hear first?'

The man said, 'Give me the bad news first.'

'Your wife has got hold of a picture worth half a million pounds!'

'That's the bad news? What could be worse than that?' asked the man.

'Well, it's a picture of you and your secretary, and now she wants a divorce.'

God bless blondes!

Blind courage

A blind man enters a Ladies' Bar by mistake. He finds his way to a bar stool and orders a drink.

After his drink arrives, he yells to the barman, 'Want to hear a blonde joke?!'

The bar immediately falls absolutely quiet.

In a very deep, husky voice, the woman next to him says, 'Before you tell that joke, sir, I think it fair, given that you're blind – there are five things you should know:

First – The bartender is a blonde girl.

Second – The bouncer is a blonde girl.

Third – I'm a six foot tall, 14 stone blonde woman with a black belt in karate.

Fourth – The woman sitting next to me is blonde and is a professional weightlifter.

And Fifth – The lady to your right is a blonde and is a professional wrestler.

Now think about it seriously, mister. Do you still wanna tell that joke?'

The blind man thinks for a second, shakes his head, and says, 'Nah ... Not if I'm gonna have to explain it five times.'

Holey trinity

A mathematician, a philosopher, and a blonde all go to Hell and receive a challenge from the Devil – if they can stump him, they're free to go to Heaven instead. The philosopher goes first and asks the Devil a very hard philosophy question, to which the Devil snaps his fingers, gets a book, and gives the correct answer. The mathematician tries as well – but the Devil instantly gets the answer. When it comes to the blonde, she pulls up a chair and drills three holes in it. She then sits down in the chair and farts.

'Now,' she says, 'which hole did the fart come out of?'

'That's easy,' says the Devil, 'all of them.'

'No, stupid!' says the blonde. 'It came out of my arse-hole!'

The ventriloquist's dummy

A ventriloquist is touring the clubs and stops to put on a show in a small town. He's going through his usual run of off-colour and dumb blonde jokes when a well-presented blonde woman in the fourth row stands up and says:

'I've heard just about enough of your stupid blonde jokes, DICKHEAD! What makes you think you can stereotype women that way? What connection can a person's hair colour possibly have with their fundamental worth as a human being? It's morons like you that prevent women like me from being respected at work and in our communities, and from reaching our full potential.'

Flustered, the ventriloquist begins to apologise, when the blonde yells, 'You stay out of this, mister. I'm talking to that little b*****d on your knee!'

Ten blondes on Everest

Eleven women were clinging precariously to a wildly swinging rope suspended from a crumbling rock on Mount Everest. Ten were blonde, one was a brunette.

As a group they decided that one of the party should let go. If that didn't happen, the rope would break and everyone would perish. For an agonising few moments nobody volunteered. Finally, the brunette gave a truly touching speech, saying she would sacrifice herself to save the lives of the others.

The blondes applauded.

Boom-boom

TGIF?

Why do blondes have TGIF written on their shoes?

Toes Go In First.

lightning smile

Why do blondes always smile during lightning storms?

They think their picture is being taken.

pin brain

What do you do if a blonde throws a pin at you?

Run, she's got a grenade in her mouth!

bird brain

A blonde and a brunette are walking outside when the brunette says, 'Oh, look at the dead bird.'

The blonde looks skyward and says, 'Where, where?'

Two blondes go bananas

Two blondes were travelling by train for
the first time. They had brought along a
bag of bananas for lunch. Just as one bit
into her banana, the train entered a
tunnel under a mountain. In the darkness
the blonde said, 'Did you take a bite of
your banana?'

'No.'

'Well, don't.

'I did and I just went blind.'

Mail domination

A man was in his front garden mowing the lawn when his attractive blonde female neighbour came out of the house and went straight to her mailbox. She opened it, then slammed it shut and stormed back into the house.

A little later, she came out of her house again, went to the mailbox and, again, opened it and then slammed it shut. Angrily, back into the house she went.

Just as the man was getting ready to edge his lawn, she came out again, marched to the mailbox, opened it and then slammed it closed harder than ever. Puzzled by her actions the man asked her, 'Is there something wrong?'

To which she replied, 'There certainly is! My stupid computer keeps saying, 'YOU'VE GOT MAIL!!!!!!!''

The cruise

A blonde is walking past a travel agent's and notices a sign in the window: 'Cruise Special – £99. This week only!'

So she goes inside, puts her money down on the counter and says, 'Is there any room left on the £99 cruise special, I would really be pleased if you could squeeze me in!'

Without a word, the agent grabs her, drags her into the back room, ties her to a large inner tube, then drags her out the back door. He then pulls her down a steep slope at the back of the shop to the river, where he pushes her in and sends her floating off.

A second blonde comes by a few minutes later, sees the sign, goes inside, lays her money on the counter, and asks for the £99 special. This blonde also suffers the same fate, being tied to an inner tube and sent floating down the river.

The currents are strong and the fast-flowing water pushes the second blonde along so quickly that she eventually catches up with the first.

They float side by side for a while, both spluttering to get the river water out of their mouths before the first blonde asks, 'Do they serve refreshments on this cruise?'

The second blonde replies, 'They didn't last year.'

Passing for brunette

A young brunette went into the doctor's office and reported that her body hurt wherever she touched it.

'Impossible,' said the doctor. 'Show me what you mean.'

So, she took her finger, pressed it against her elbow and screamed in agony. Then she pressed her knee and screamed, pressed her ankle and screamed and so it went on. Everywhere she touched made her scream.

Finally, the doctor said, 'You're not really a brunette, are you?'

'No, I'm actually a blonde,' she replied.

'I thought so,' said the doctor. 'Your finger is broken.'

The job interview

A young blonde woman goes to an office for a job interview. The interviewer decides to start with the basics. 'So, miss, can you tell us your age, please?'

The blonde counts carefully on her fingers for about three seconds before replying, 'Err ... 23!'

The interviewer tries another straightforward question to break the ice. 'And can you tell us your height, please?'

The young lady stands up and produces a measuring tape from her handbag. She traps one end under her foot and extends the tape to the top of her head. She checks the measurement and announces, 'Five foot three!'

This isn't looking good so the interviewer goes for the real basics. 'And, err, just to confirm for our records, your name please?'

The blonde bobs her head from side to side for about 20 seconds, mouthing something silently to herself, before finally replying, 'Stephanie.'

The interviewer is completely baffled at this stage, so he asks, 'Just out of curiosity, miss. We can understand your counting on your fingers to work out your age, and the measuring tape for your height is obvious, but what were you doing when we asked you your name?'

'Ohh that!' replies the blonde. 'That's just me running through 'Happy birthday to you, happy birthday to you …''

Father and son

Taking a back seat

Tom had just passed his driving test. To celebrate, the whole family trooped out to the driveway and climbed into the car for his inaugural drive. His dad immediately headed to the back seat, directly behind the newly minted driver.

'I'll bet you're back there to get a change of scenery after all those months of sitting in the front passenger seat teaching me how to drive,' said the beaming boy to his dad.

'No,' came his dad's reply, 'I'm going to sit here and kick the back of your seat as you drive, just like you've been doing to me for seventeen years.'

Simple tastes

Five-year-old Johnny was lost, so he went up to a policeman and said, 'I've lost my dad!'

The policeman said, 'What's he like?'

Little Johnny replied, 'Beer and women!'

It's a miracle!

A boy and his father from the country were visiting a shopping centre for the first time. They were amazed by almost everything they saw, but especially by two shiny, silver walls that could move apart and then slide back together again. The boy asked, 'What is that, father?'

The father (never having seen a lift) responded, 'Son, I have never seen anything like this in my life. I don't know what it is.'

While the boy and his father were watching in amazement, a fat old lady in a wheelchair rolled up to the moving walls and pressed a button. The walls opened and the lady rolled between them into a small room. The walls closed and the boy and his father watched the small circular numbers above the walls light up sequentially. They continued to watch until the last number was reached and then the numbers began to light up in reverse order. Finally, the walls opened up again and a gorgeous, voluptuous 24-year-old blonde woman stepped out. The father, not taking his eyes off the young woman, said quietly to his son, 'Go get your mother.'

For richer for poorer

A little boy asked his father, 'Daddy, how much does it cost to get married?'

His father replied, 'I don't know son, I'm still paying.'

Childhood is so precious

A father asked his son, little Jimmy, if he knew about the birds and the bees.

'I don't want to know!' little Jimmy said, exploding and bursting into tears.

Confused, his father asked little Jimmy what was wrong.

'Dad,' Jimmy sobbed, 'for me there was no Father Christmas at age six, no Easter Bunny at age seven, and no Tooth Fairy at age eight. And if you're telling me now that grown-ups really don't f***, I've got nothing left to believe in!'

Whole lotta woman

A little boy is in a supermarket queue with his dad. In front of them is a really fat woman. The little boy looks her over, turns to his dad and says, 'She is really big and fat isn't she Daddy?'

The father is embarrassed and tries to get his son to quieten down. A few minutes later, the little boy yells out, 'She's the biggest woman I have ever seen!'

The father is mortified, and bends over and tells his son, 'We do not talk about people looking different from us, especially if they are fat. Don't do it again.'

The little boy gets the message and stands quietly for a while, until the woman's pager goes off. Then yells out, 'Look out Daddy, she's reversing!'

Driven to drink

Jet propelled

A couple of aeroplane mechanics are in a hangar at the airport.

It's foggy and as all the planes are grounded, they have nothing to do. One mechanic says to the other, 'Dave, have you got anything to drink?'

Dave says, 'Nah mate, but I hear you can drink jet fuel, and it will give you a buzz.'

So they drink some jet fuel, and very soon they are rolling around the hangar, singing and having a whale of a time!

The following morning, Dave's mate wakes up and he just knows his head will explode if he gets up ... but it doesn't. He gets up and feels good. In fact, he feels great! No hangover!

The phone rings. It's Dave. Dave says, 'Hey, how do you feel?'

'Great!' he says. 'Just great!'

Dave says, 'Yeah, I feel great too, and no hangover. That jet fuel stuff is the business. We should do this more often!'

'Yeah, we could, but there's just one thing ...'

'What's that?'

'Have you farted yet?'

'No ...'

'Well, DON'T, 'cos I'm in f***ing France.'

Be careful what you wish for

Two Frenchmen, Pierre and Michel, were adrift in a lifeboat following a dramatic escape from a burning freighter.

While rummaging through the boat's provisions, Pierre stumbled across an old lamp. Secretly hoping that a genie would appear, he rubbed the lamp vigorously. To his amazement, a genie indeed came forth.

This particular genie, however, stated that he could only deliver one wish, not the standard three. Without giving much thought to the matter, Pierre blurted out, 'Turn the entire ocean into red wine!'

The genie clapped his hands with a deafening crash, and immediately the entire sea turned into wine of the finest vintage ever sampled by mortals. Simultaneously, the genie vanished.

Only the gentle lapping of wine on the hull broke the stillness as the two men considered their circumstances. Michel looked disgustedly at Pierre, whose wish had been granted. After a long, tension-filled moment, he spoke: 'Nice going Pierre. Now we're going to have to p*ss in the boat.'

In vino veritas

A drunken driver was pulled over by the police. The policeman said to him, 'Excuse me, sir, but you appeared to be driving rather erratically. Would you mind blowing into this breathalyser?'

The drunk said, 'I can't do that.'

The policeman said, 'And why not sir?'

'I suffer from very acute asthma and blowing like that could kill me,' he replied.

The policeman said, 'Very well, sir, you will have to accompany me to the police station and give a urine sample.'

The drunk said, 'I can't do that.'

The policeman said, 'And why not, sir?'

The drunk said, 'Because I suffer from a rare kidney disease, and forcing myself to p*ss could do me untold damage.'

The policeman said, 'That's no problem, sir, we can take a blood sample instead.'

The drunk said, 'I can't do that.'

The policeman said, 'And why can't you give a blood sample?'

The drunk said, 'Because I have a severely weakened heart, and giving even a small amount of blood could kill me.'

The policeman radioed his sergeant at the station and asked for his advice. The sergeant said, 'You'll have to revert to the old method. Draw a chalk line and get him to walk along it.'

The sergeant drew a chalk line on the road, then said to the drunk, 'Right, sir, I want you to walk along that line as straight as you can.'

The drunk said, 'I can't do that.'

The policeman, now irate, said, 'And why the hell can't you walk along the line?'

'Because I'm p*ssed,' said the drunk.

The competition

A man walks into a pub and says to the landlord, 'A pint of beer, please.'

As the landlord is pulling the pint, the man notices a large bottle filled with £20 notes, so he says to the landlord, 'Tell me, what's the bottle of £20 notes for?'

The landlord says, 'That's for a competition we have.'

The man says, 'What competition is that?'

The landlord says, 'The competition consists of three tasks. Anyone who can complete the tasks, gets the bottle of £20 notes.'

The man says, 'And what tasks might they be?'

The landlord says, 'Well, you see the big bloke at the door. You have to knock him out with one punch. That's the first task.'

The man says, 'Oh! He's a hell of a size. What's the second task?'

The landlord says, 'The second task is a little harder. At the back of the pub there's an Alsatian with a bad tooth, and it's in one hell of a temper. You have to pull its tooth out.'

The man says, 'That sounds dangerous. What's the third task?'

The landlord says, 'There's a woman called Mary who works in the kitchen. She's not had sex for 20 years. You have to satisfy her and make her happy. If you want to try your luck at the competition it will cost you £20.'

The man says, 'I don't think I'll bother.'

A while later, after he's had a few pints, the man looks at the bottle of £20 notes, then at the big bloke and says to himself, 'He doesn't look as big as he did when I first came in.'

He shouts to the landlord and says, 'I'll have a go at the tasks.' He gives the landlord £20, walks over to the big bloke, gives him one hell of a punch and knocks him clean out.

Then he says, 'Right, now for task two.' He goes out to the back of the pub. About 20 minutes later he comes back in, all his clothes ripped, covered in blood and scratches, and says, 'Right, where's the woman with the bad tooth?'

Hello my ducks

A bloke goes into a pub holding three ducks. He puts them on the bar and orders a drink.

After drinking a couple of pints and chatting to the landlord for a while, the man excuses himself and heads off for the gents.

The landlord feels a tad awkward with just himself and the three ducks at the bar, so he decides to have a go at making small-talk with them.

He asks the first duck, 'What's your name?'

'Huey,' replies the duck.

'So, how's your day been?'

'Oh, I've had a great day thanks,' replies Huey. 'I've been up to the park and in and out of puddles all day.'

The landlord asks the second duck, 'What's your name?'

'Duey,' replies the duck.

'So, how's your day been?'

'Oh, I've had a great day too thanks,' replies Duey. 'I've been up to the park and in and out of puddles all day.'

The witty landlord says to the third duck, 'So I guess your name is Louie?'

The duck replies, 'No, I'm Puddles.'

Getting ratted

A man walks into a pub and asks the landlord, 'If I show you a really good trick, will you give me a free drink?' The landlord considers the proposition, then agrees. The man reaches into his pocket and pulls out a tiny rat. He reaches into his other pocket and pulls out a tiny piano. The rat stretches, cracks his knuckles, and proceeds to play the blues.

When the man has finished his free drink, he asks the landlord, 'If I show you an even better trick, will you give me free drinks for the rest of the evening?' The landlord agrees, thinking that no trick could possibly be better than the first one.

The man reaches into his pocket and pulls out the tiny rat again. He reaches into his other pocket and, again, pulls out the tiny piano. Once again, the rat stretches, cracks his knuckles, and proceeds to play the blues. The man reaches into another pocket and pulls out a small bullfrog, who begins to sing along with the rat's music.

While the man is enjoying his beverages, a stranger confronts him and offers him £100,000 for the bullfrog. 'Sorry,' the man replies, 'he's not for sale.' The stranger increases the offer to £250,000 cash up front. 'No,' he insists, 'he's not for sale.' The stranger again increases the offer, this time to £500,000 cash. The man finally agrees, and turns the frog over to the stranger in exchange for the money.

'Are you insane?' the landlord demands. 'That frog could have been worth millions to you, and you let him go for a mere £500,000!'

'Don't worry about it,' the man answers. 'The frog was really nothing special. You see, the rat's a ventriloquist.'

Drunk

A guy stumbled in through the front door of a bar completely drunk. He walked up to the barman and asked for a drink. The barman kindly told the guy he couldn't give him a drink because he was already drunk. Angry, the guy stumbled back out the front door.

About five minutes later, the guy stumbled in through the side door of the bar. He asked the barman for a drink and once again the barman told the guy no because he was already drunk. The guy stumbled back out through the side door.

A few minutes later, the guy stumbled in through the back door of the bar. He walked up to the bar, looked at the barman for a moment then said, 'Damn, man, how many bars do you work at?'

Head games

A brain walks into a pub and says, 'I'll have a pint of beer please.'

The barman looks at him and says 'Sorry, I can't serve you.'

'Why not?' asks the brain.

'You're already out of your head.'

What a curry on!

Vinda-loo?

A man goes down the pub promising faithfully to his wife he'll be back by 11pm. One drink leads to two, then another, and eventually he rolls in at 3am. He falls in the door blind drunk, crawling and stumbling about. The last thing he remembers is finding the remains of a take-away curry in the kitchen. It's stone cold, the meat is in dried-up lumps and the sauce is disgusting, but he's so hungry he eats it anyway.

Next morning he wakes up with a thumping head and a churning stomach, but that's nothing to the roasting he knows he'll get from his wife. The first thing he says to her is, 'Sorry about last night, darling.'

She replies, 'That's all right. I was really mad at you but I've forgiven you now I've seen that you cleaned the cat's litter tray out when you came in last night.'

A sick joke

This bloke arrives home to find his wife waiting for him by the door.

'And what time do you call this,' she says angrily. 'You went down to the take-away three hours ago, and now you stagger back here stinking of booze, with no food!'

'Look,' the bloke responds calmly, 'How do you fancy a chicken vindaloo, rice, Bombay potatoes and a chapatti?'

'Oh, all right then,' his now really hungry wife agrees.

'Fine,' he says, and throws up all over her!

Bohemian crapsody

to be sung to the tune of Queen's
'Bohemian Rhapsody'

Naan-aa, just killed a man
Poppadom against his head
Had lime pickle, now he's dead.
Naan-aa, my meal had just begun
But now I'm going to crap it all away.
Naan-aa, ooh-oo-oo-ooh,
Didn't mean to make you cry,
Seen nothin' yet just see the loo
   tomorrow,
Curry on, curry on, cos nothing really
   madras.

Too late, my dinner's gone,
Sends shivers up my spine,
Rectum's aching all the time.
Goodbye every bhaji, I've got to go,
Gotta leave you all behind and use the loo.
Naan-aa, ooh-oo-oo-ooh,

This dopiaza's mild,
I sometimes wish we'd never come here
   at all.

******

[Guitar solo]

******

I see a little chicken tikka on the side,
Rogan josh, rogan josh, pass the chutney
   made of mango.
Vindaloo does nicely.
Very very spicy ME!
Biryani (biryani).
Biryani (biryani).
Biryani and a naan.
(A vindaloo loo loo-oo …)
I've eaten balti, somebody help me.
He's eaten balti, get him to a lavatory.
Stand you well back, cos this loo is
   quarantined.

Here it comes.
There it goes.
Technicolor yawn.
I chunder.
No!
It's coming up again.
(There he goes) I chunder.

It's coming up again.
(There he goes) it's coming up again
    (up again).
Coming up again (up again).
Here it comes again.
(No no no no no no no no no NO!)
On my knees, I'm on my knees, I'm on
    my knees.
Oh there he goes.
This vindaloo
Is about to wreck my guts.
Poor me ... poor me ... poor me!

******

[Guitar solo]

******

So you think you can chunder and still it's
    all right?
So you want to eat curry and drink beer
    all night?
Ohh maybe, now you'll puke like a baby,
Just had to come out,
Just had to come right out in here.

******

[Guitar solo]

******

Korma, saag or bhuna,
Balti, naan, bhaji.
Nothing makes a difference,
Nothing makes a difference to me.

(Anyway, my wind blows.)

Down the pan

**Personality types you might meet in
the gents**

excitable

Shorts half twisted around, can't find
hole, rips shorts.

sociable

Joins friends in peeing whether he has
to or not.

cross-eyed

Looks into next urinal to see how the other bloke's fixed.

timid

Can't pee if someone is watching, flushes urinal and comes back later.

indifferent

If all urinals being used, pees in sink.

clever

No hands, adjusts tie, looks around and pees on floor.

worried

Not sure of where he has been lately, makes quick inspection.

frivolous

Aims stream up, down and across urinal, tries to hit fly or bug.

absent-minded

Opens jacket, pulls out tie, pees in pants.

childish

Pees directly in bottom of urinal, likes to see it bubble.

tough

Bangs penis on side of urinal to dry it.

patient

Stands very close for a long time, waiting, lets it drip dry, reads with other hand.

efficient

Waits until he has to crap, then does both.

drunk

Holds left thumb in right hand, pees in pants.

disgruntled

Stands for a while, gives up, walks away.

conceited

Holds two-inch penis like a baseball bat.

desperate

Waits in long line, teeth clenched, pees in pants.

sneaky

Farts silently while peeing, acts very innocent, knows man in next stall will get the blame.

Gentlemen of leisure

Ten sure-fire ways to entertain the bloke
in the next cubicle

1 Grunt and strain really loudly for
30 seconds, then drop a melon into
the toilet bowl from a height of six
feet. Sigh in a relaxed fashion.

2 Fill up a large flask with Lucozade.
Squirt it erratically under the cubicle
walls of your neighbours while yelling,
'Whoa! Easy, big boy!'

3 Cheer and clap loudly every time
somebody breaks the silence with a
bodily function noise.

4 Using a small squeezable tube,
spread peanut butter on a wad of
toilet paper. Drop the wad under the
cubicle wall of your neighbour, then
say, 'Whoops, could you kick that
back over here please?'

5 Say, 'C'mon Mr Happy! Don't fall asleep on me!'

6 Drop a D-cup bra on the floor under the divider where the person in the next cubicle can see it.

7 Say, 'Damn, this water's cold!'

8 Say, 'Hmm, I've never seen that colour before.'

9 Say, 'Interesting, more floaters than sinkers.'

10 Drop a marble and say, 'Oh noooo, my glass eye!'

Boys' toys

An acceptable excuse for speeding

A man, on reaching his fortieth birthday, decided it was time to buy the car he had always wanted. After touring around several garages to get the best deal, he eventually purchased a top-of-the-range sports hatch.

The man decided to take his new car for a spin and headed out that evening to see how it would perform on some country lanes near his home.

The top was down, the breeze was blowing through what was left of his hair, and he decided to open her up.

As the needle jumped up to 80mph, he suddenly saw flashing red and blue lights behind him.

'There's no way they can catch this car,' he thought to himself and opened her up further. The needle hit 90, 100 as he continued to weave round the bends and sped away from the police car ... then the reality of the situation hit him.

'What the hell am I doing?' he thought and pulled over.

The man tentatively lowered the window, as the policeman sauntered over to the car and let out a heavy, long-suffering sigh.

The policeman took his licence without a word, and examined it and the car. 'It's been a long day, this is the end of my shift, and it's Friday 13th. I don't feel like more paperwork, so if you can give me an excuse for your driving that I haven't heard before, you can go.'

The driver thought for a second and said, 'Last week my wife ran off with a policeman. I was afraid you were trying to give her back.'

'Have a nice weekend,' said the officer.

A question of priorities

A young hot-shot in the City parks his brand new Porsche in front of the office to show it off to his colleagues. Just as he's getting out of the car, a truck comes speeding along too close to the kerb and rips off the door before speeding away.

More than a little distraught, the man grabs his mobile and calls the police. Five minutes later, the police arrive. Before the policeman has a chance to ask any questions, the man starts screaming hysterically, 'My Porsche, my beautiful silver Porsche is ruined. No matter how long the panel beaters work at it, it'll simply never be the same again!'

When the man has finally finished his rant, the policeman shakes his head in disgust. 'I can't believe how materialistic you City workers are,' he says. 'You lot are so focused on your possessions that you don't notice anything else in your life.'

'How can you say such a thing at a time like this?' snaps the man.

The policeman replies, 'Didn't you realise that your right arm was torn off when the truck hit you?'

The man looks down in absolute horror. 'F***ing' hell!' he screams. 'Where's my Rolex?!'

The finer things in life

A man entered his favourite ritzy restaurant and, while sitting at his regular table, situated so that he could view the new arrivals, noticed a gorgeous woman sitting at a table nearby, all alone.

He called the waiter over and asked for their most expensive bottle of Merlot to be sent over to her, knowing that if she accepted it, she would be his.

The waiter got the bottle and quickly took it over to the lady, saying, 'This is from the gentleman over there. He would like you to accept it with his compliments.'

She looked at the wine and decided to send a note over to the man.

The note read, 'For me to accept this bottle, you need to have a Mercedes in your garage, a million pounds in the bank, and seven inches in your pants.'

The man read the note and sent one of his own back to her. It read, 'Just so you know – I happen to have a Ferrari Testarossa, an 8 series BMW and a Mercedes convertible in my garage; plus I have over 20 million pounds in the bank; but, even for a woman as beautiful as you, I would never cut three inches off my d*ck. Just send the bottle back.'

Sexploits

No excuse

A husband emerged naked from the bathroom after performing his nightly ablutions, and came into the bedroom.

He was climbing into bed when his wife began complaining, as usual with another list of excuses, 'I know you're not going to believe this, Dave, but, the kids spent two hours this evening running around the house, pretending they were having an intergalactic war with their water pistols; my boss was shouting at me to finish all his filing, again, and I've spent three hours doing the ironing – it's all given me a dreadful headache.'

'Perfect,' said her husband. 'I was just in the bathroom powdering my knob with aspirin. You can take it orally or as a suppository, it's up to you!'

Doing it by the book

A bloke sitting in a pub notices a woman reading a book. He leans over towards her a little so he can see the title and notes that it's about penises. He walks over to her and says, 'That book looks interesting.'

The woman says, 'Yes it is. It's full of facts. Did you know that the Native American has the fattest penis and that Polish men have the longest penises?'

The bloke says, 'No I didn't know that. Look, can I buy you a drink?'

The woman says, 'Yes, I'll have a drink, but we should introduce ourselves first. My name's Mary. Pleased to meet you.'

The bloke says, 'Hello, Mary. My name's Tonto Kolowski!'

Mustn't grumble

This bloke has been out with his mates for the evening watching porn films, and all the sexual moans and groans have got him excited.

On arriving home, he jumps into bed and starts fondling his wife, then he gets on top of her and starts to make love. But his wife is half asleep and just lies there.

The bloke says to his wife, 'How come you don't moan and groan like other women?'

His wife says, 'All right, if that's what you want. LOOK AT THE STATE OF THIS BEDROOM, THAT CEILING COULD DO WITH PAINTING AND THE CARPET COULD DO WITH CHANGING!'

Research findings

In 2003, the UK government funded a study to see why the head of a man's penis is larger than the shaft. After one year and £180,000, the study concluded that the reason the head was larger than the shaft was to give a man more pleasure during sexual intercourse.

After the UK government had published its findings, the French decided to do their own study. After £250,000 and three years of research, they concluded that the reason the head was larger than the shaft was to give the woman more pleasure during sexual intercourse.

Australian scientists, unsatisfied with these conclusions, conducted their own study. After two weeks and a cost of £54.95, they concluded that it was to keep a man's hand from flying off and hitting him in the eye.

The German and the prostitute

A German bloke on a visit to England has the evening to kill and as he is on his own, decides to find the red-light district in the city.

After looking on his A-Z for the names of streets that his colleagues have mentioned on similar trips, he manages to find his way to a shady-looking area.

Approaching a lady who looks like she may be able to give him a good time, he says, 'I vish to buy sex wit you.'

'OK, that'll be £20,' says the girl.

'Goot, but I'm a liddle kinky.'

'No problem,' says the girl.

Off they go to her flat. When they get inside, the German produces four large bedsprings and one of those whistles that makes a noise like a duck.

'Tie zeese springs to your hans und knees,' the German demands.

The girl finds this odd but does as he asks. 'Now you vill get on your hands und knees und you vill blow zis vistle as I make love to you.'

The sex is fantastic! She's bouncing all over the room honking on the duck caller. The climax is the most sensational she's ever had and it's several minutes before she recovers her breath to ask, 'What do you call that?'

'Ah,' says the German, 'four-sprung duck technique.'

Nightmare 1

After a long night of making love, a young
bloke rolled over, pulled out a cigarette
from his jeans and searched for his lighter.
Unable to find it, he asked the girl he was
with if she had one to hand.

'There might be some matches in the top
drawer,' she replied.

He opened the drawer of the bedside
table and found a box of matches sitting
neatly on top of a framed picture of
another man. Naturally, the bloke began to
worry. 'Is this your husband?' he enquired
nervously.

'No, silly,' she replied, snuggling up to him.

'Your boyfriend then?' he asked.

'No, not at all,' she said, nibbling away at
his ear.

'Well, who is he then?' demanded the
bewildered bloke.

Calmly, the girl replied, 'That's me before
the operation.'

Nightmare 2

One night a bloke takes his girlfriend home. As they are about to kiss each other goodnight at the front door, the bloke starts feeling a little horny. With an air of confidence, he leans with his hand against the wall and, smiling, he says to her, 'Would you give me a blow job, darling?'

Horrified, she replies, 'Are you mad? My parents will see us!'

'Oh, come on! Who's going to see us at this hour?' he asks, grinning at her.

'No, please. Can you imagine if we got caught?'

'Oh, come on! There's nobody around – they're all sleeping!'

'No way. It's just too risky!'

'Oh, please, please. I love you so much.'

'No, no and no. I love you too, but I just can't!'

'Oh yes you can. Please?'

Out of the blue, the light on the stairs comes on, and the girl's sister opens the door in her pyjamas, hair dishevelled, and in a sleepy voice she says, 'Dad says to go ahead and give him a blow job, or I can do it, or if need be, Mum says she can come down herself and do it. But for God's sake tell him to take his hand off the intercom!'

Italian stallion

A virile young Italian soldier was relaxing at his favourite bar in Rome, when he managed to attract a spectacular young blonde. Things progressed to the point where he invited her back to his apartment and, after some small-talk, they had sex.

After a pleasant interlude, he asked with a smile, 'So ... you finish?' She paused for a second, frowned, and replied, 'No.'

Surprised, the young man reached for her, and the f***ing resumed. This time, she thrashed about wildly, and there were screams of passion. The sex ended, and again, the young man smiled, and asked, 'You finish?' And again, after a short pause, she returned his smile, cuddled closer to him, and softly said, 'No.'

Stunned, but damned if this woman was going to outlast him, the young man reached for the woman. Using the last of his strength, he barely managed it; but they climaxed simultaneously, screaming, bucking, clawing and ripping the bed sheets.

The exhausted man fell on to his back, gasping. Barely able to turn his head, he looked into her eyes, smiled proudly, and asked, 'You finish?'

'No!' she smiled back, 'I Sveedish!'

Charging for it

A boy and his date were parked on a back road some distance from town, doing what boys and girls do on back roads, when the girl stopped the boy. 'I really should have mentioned this earlier, but I'm actually a prostitute and I charge £20 for sex.'

The boy reluctantly paid her, and they did their thing. After a cigarette, the boy just sat in the driver's seat looking out the window.

'Why aren't we going anywhere?' asked the girl.

'Well, I should have mentioned this before, but I'm actually a taxi driver, and the fare back to town is £25.'

Oops

A girl asks her boyfriend to come over Friday night and have dinner with her parents. Since this is such a big event, the girl announces to her boyfriend that, after dinner, she would like to go out and make love for the first time.

The boy is ecstatic, but he has never had sex before, so he takes a trip to the pharmacist to get some condoms. The pharmacist helps the boy for about an hour. He tells the boy everything there is to know about condoms and sex. At the cash register, the pharmacist asks the boy how many condoms he'd like to buy: a 3-pack, 10-pack or a family pack.

'I'm really going to put it to this girl,' the boy tells the pharmacist.

The pharmacist, with a laugh, suggests the family pack, saying the boy will be rather busy, it being his first time.

That night, the boy shows up at the girl's parents' house and meets his girlfriend at the door. 'Oh, I'm so excited for you to meet my parents, come on in!'

The boy goes inside and is taken to the dinner table where the girl's parents are seated. The boy quickly offers to say grace and bows his head. A minute passes, and the boy is still deep in prayer with his head down. Ten minutes pass, and still no movement from the boy. Finally, after twenty minutes with his head down, the girlfriend leans over and whispers to the boyfriend, 'I had no idea you were this religious.'

The boy turns, and whispers back, 'I had no idea your father was a pharmacist.'

Lethal weapon

A woman pregnant with triplets was walking down the street when a masked robber ran out of a bank and shot her three times in the stomach. Luckily the babies were all right. The surgeon decided to leave the bullets in because it was too risky to operate. In the fullness of time the woman gave birth to two healthy daughters and a healthy son.

All was fine for 16 years, and then one daughter walked into the room in tears. 'What's wrong?' asked the mother.

'I was taking a tinkle and this bullet came out,' replied the daughter. The mother told her it was OK and explained what had happened 16 years ago.

About a week later, the second daughter walked into the room in tears. 'Mum, I was taking a tinkle and this bullet came out.' Again the mother told her not to worry and explained what had happened 16 years ago.

A week later, her son walked into the room in tears. 'It's OK,' said the mum, 'I know what happened, you were taking a tinkle and a bullet came out.'

'No,' said the boy, 'I was playing with myself and I shot the dog ...'

Keeping it up

A man walks into a pharmacy, looking around nervously and intently examines all the shelves before sidling up to the counter.

Eventually, he approaches the pharmacist and says, 'Listen, I have three girls coming over tonight. I've never had three girls at once, so I need something to keep me horny ... potent.'

The pharmacist tries not to smile and reaches under the counter, unlocks the bottom drawer and takes out a small cardboard box marked with a label, 'Sexual stimulants – extra strength' and says, 'Here, if you eat these blue pills, you'll go nuts for twelve hours.'

'Give me three boxes,' pleads the man eagerly, and digs out his cash and pays for the pills.

The next day, the man walks into the same pharmacy, and seeing there is nobody else around, limps straight up to the counter and pulls down his pants. The pharmacist looks in horror as he notices the man's penis is black and blue, and the skin is hanging off in some places.

In a pained voice, the man moans out, 'Gimme a bottle of Warm Heat muscle rub.'

The pharmacist replies in horror, 'You can't put Warm Heat on that!'

The man replies, 'No, it's for my arms. The girls didn't show up.'

Animal passion

Down on the farm

A ventriloquist is out walking in Wales
when he spots a farmer stroking a
horse, and by his side are a dog and a
sheep.

The ventriloquist thinks, I'll have a bit of fun here. He walks over to the farmer and says, 'Do you mind if I have a chat with the animals?'

The farmer looks at him and says, 'Don't be stupid, they can't speak.'

The ventriloquist strokes the horse's nose and says, 'Hello, Mr Horse, how are you?'

The reply comes back, 'I'm fine, thank you.'

The farmer just stands there amazed.

Then the ventriloquist says, 'Is this your owner?'

The horse replies, 'Yes.'

Then the ventriloquist goes on to say, 'And how does he treat you?'

The horse says, 'He treats me good. He feeds me, he grooms me and he rides me now and again for exercise.'

The farmer is just dumbstruck.

The ventriloquist then turns to the dog, strokes it and says, 'Hello, Mr Dog.'

The dog replies, 'Hello.'

Again the farmer stands there astounded.

The ventriloquist says, 'Is this your owner?'

The dog replies, 'Yes, it is.'

'And how does he treat you?' says the ventriloquist.

The dog replies, 'He treats me well. He washes me, grooms me, feeds me and everywhere he goes, he takes me.'

The ventriloquist turns to the sheep, strokes it and says, 'Hello, Mr Sheep.'

Before the ventriloquist can go any further, the farmer interrupts and says, 'I wouldn't listen to what the sheep says if I were you – the sheep tells lies.'

Always let your conscience be your guide

Dave had felt guilty all day long. No matter how much he tried to forget about it, he couldn't. The guilt and sense of betrayal were overwhelming. But every once in a while he'd hear that soothing voice trying to reassure him:

'Dave, don't worry about it. You weren't the first doctor to sleep with one of your patients and you won't be the last. And you're single. Let it go!'

But invariably the other voice would bring him back to reality:

'Dave, you're a vet.'

Stuff and nonsense

This English bloke is travelling through the outback of Australia doing a little research, when he comes across a small town with a pub.

He enters the pub and it's full of sheep and cattle herders who instantly go quiet upon his entry. He walks up to the bar and orders a beer, then goes and sits at a table on his own.

One of the locals walks up and sits at the table with him and says, 'Are you a pom?'

The Englishman says, 'Yes.'

The local says, 'What you doing around here?'

The Englishman says, 'I'm on holiday and doing a little research at the same time.'

The local says, 'You a scientist or something?'

The Englishman says, 'No, I'm a taxidermist.'

The local says, 'What's a taxidermist?'

The Englishman says, 'I stuff and mount animals.'

The local turns to his mates and shouts out: 'IT'S ALL RIGHT LADS, HE'S ONE OF US!'

A moral tale

A chicken and a horse are playing together in a farmyard. Suddenly, the horse falls into a pit. He yells to the chicken, 'Go get the farmer! Save me! Save me!' The chicken goes looking for the farmer, but can't find him. So she gets into the farmer's convertible, drives over to the mud pit, lassoes the horse, ties it to the car and pulls him out.

The horse says, 'Thank you, thank you. I owe you my life ...'

Then, a couple of days later they are playing there again and this time the chicken falls into the mud pit and the chicken says, 'Help me. Help me! Go get the farmer!'

So the horse says, 'No, I think I can get to you. The horse stretches across the mud pit and tells the chicken, 'Grab onto my d*ck.' The chicken grabs on, the horse stretches back and the horse saves the chicken's life.

So, what is the moral of this story?

If you have a d*ck the size of a horse, then you don't need a flash car to pick up chicks.

Older and wiser?

Wonderful for his age

An 85-year-old man married a lovely 25-year-old woman.

Because her new husband was so old the woman decided that on their wedding night they should have separate suites. She was very worried that the old fellow might over-exert himself.

After the festivities, she prepared herself for bed and for the knock on the door she was expecting. Sure enough, the knock came and there was her groom ready for action. They came together in conjugal union and all went well, whereupon he took his leave of her and she prepared to go to sleep for the night.

After a few minutes, there was another knock on the door and there the old bloke was again, ready for some more action. Somewhat surprised, she consented to a further coupling, which was again successful, after which the octogenarian bade her a fond goodnight and left.

She was certainly ready for slumber at this point, and was close to sleep for the second time when there was another knock at the door and there he was again fresh as a 21-year-old and ready for more. Once again they did the horizontal boogie.

As they were bathing in the afterglow, the young bride said to him, 'I am really impressed that a bloke your age has enough juice to go for it three times. I've been with guys less than half your age who were only good for one.'

The old bloke looked puzzled, turned to her and said, 'Was I already here?'

As old as you feel

A man decided to have a face-lift for his birthday. He spent £5000 and felt really good about the result. On his way home, he stopped at a newsagent's and bought himself a newspaper. Before leaving, he said to the girl on the till, 'I hope you don't mind me asking, but how old do you think I am?'

'About 35,' was the reply.

'I'm actually 47,' the man said, feeling really happy.

After that, he went into the burger bar for lunch, and asked the order-taker the same question, to which the reply was, 'Oh, you look about 29.'

'I am actually 47!' This made him feel really good.

While standing at the bus stop he asked an old woman the same question. She replied, 'I am 85 years old and my eyesight is going. But when I was young there was a sure way of telling a man's age. If I put my hand in your pants and play with you for ten minutes I will be able to tell your exact age.'

As there was no one around, the man thought 'what the hell', and let her slip her hand into his pants.

Ten minutes later, the old lady said, 'OK, it's done. You are 47.'

Stunned, the man said, 'That was brilliant! How did you do that?'

Grinning, the old lady replied, 'I was behind you in the burger bar.'

Failing powers

A 75-year-old man went to the doctor's surgery to get a sperm count. The doctor gave the man a jar and said, 'Take this jar home and bring me back a semen sample tomorrow.'

The next day, the 75-year-old man reappeared at the doctor's surgery and gave him the jar, which was as clean and empty as on the previous day. The doctor asked what happened and the man explained, 'Well, doctor, it's like this. First I tried with my right hand, but nothing. Then I tried with my left hand, but still nothing. Then I asked my wife for help. She tried with her right hand, then her left, still nothing. She even tried with her mouth, first with her teeth in, then with her teeth out, and still nothing. We even called up Mavis, the lady who lives next door, and she tried too, first with both hands, then an armpit, and she even tried squeezing it between her knees, but still nothing.'

The doctor was shocked. 'You asked your NEIGHBOUR?'

'Oh yes,' the old man replied, 'but no matter what we tried, we still couldn't get the damn jar open!'

Fully functional?

Three men were sitting on the steps of
the nursing home discussing ageing.

'60 is the worst age to be,' announced
the 60 year old. 'You always feel like
you have to pee. And most of the time,
you stand at the toilet and nothing
comes out.'

'Ah, that's nothing,' said the 70 year old.
'When you're 70, you can't take a sh*t
any more. You have to take laxatives, eat
bran – you sit on the toilet all day and
nothing comes out!'

'Actually,' said the 80 year old, '80 is the
worst age of all.'

'Do you have trouble peeing too?' asked
the 60 year old.

'No … not really. I pee every morning at
6am. I pee like a racehorse – no problem
at all.'

'Do you have trouble taking a dump?' asked the 70 year old.

'No, not really. I have a great bowel movement every morning at 6.30.'

With great exasperation, the 60 year old said, 'Let me get this straight. You pee every morning at 6 o'clock and take a sh*t every morning at 6.30. What's so tough about being 80?'

The 80 year old replied, 'I don't wake up until 10.'

Football crazy

Life goes on ...

Bob receives a free ticket to the Cup Final from his company.

He plans a big weekend out, travelling down the night before to meet some mates who live nearby for a few beers and then getting up early to spend the morning savouring the atmosphere in some more local hostelries before heading off to the stadium.

Unfortunately, when he gets to the stadium, he realises his seat's in the last row in the corner of the stands, without much of a view.

After wandering around, getting a drink and a burger, Bob notices an empty seat near the half-way line and just ten rows back from the pitch. He decides to take a chance and walks all the way down, avoiding the security guards, to snatch the empty seat.

As he sits down, he asks the bloke next to him, 'Excuse me, is anyone sitting here?'

The man says, 'No.'

Excited to be in such a great seat for the game, Bob shouts, 'This is incredible! Who in their right mind would have a seat like this for the Cup Final and not use it?!'

The man replies, 'Well, actually, the seat belongs to me. I was supposed to come with my wife, but she passed away. This is the first Cup Final we haven't been to together since we got married in 1967.'

'That's really sad,' said Bob, 'but, still, couldn't you find someone to take the seat? A relative or a close friend?'

'No,' the man replied, 'they're all at the funeral.'

Einstein, Picasso and Beckham

Albert Einstein died and went to Heaven. At the pearly gates, St Peter told him, 'You look like Einstein, but you have NO idea the lengths that some people will go to to sneak into Heaven. Can you prove who you really are?'

Einstein pondered for a few seconds and asked, 'Could I have a blackboard and some chalk?'

St Peter snapped his fingers and a blackboard and chalk instantly appeared. Einstein proceeded to describe, with arcane mathematics and symbols, his theory of relativity. St Peter was suitably impressed. 'You really ARE Einstein,' he said. 'Welcome to Heaven!'

The next to arrive was Pablo Picasso. Once again, St Peter asked for credentials. Picasso asked, 'Mind if I use that blackboard and chalk?'

'Go ahead,' said St Peter. Picasso erased Einstein's equations and sketched a truly stunning mural with just a few strokes of chalk. St Peter applauded. 'Surely you are the great artist you claim to be,' he said. 'Come on in!'

Then St Peter looked up and saw David Beckham standing there. St Peter scratched his head and said, 'Einstein and Picasso both managed to prove their identity. How can you prove yours?'

Beckham looked bewildered and said, 'Who are Einstein and Picasso?'

'Come on in, David.'

Don't you know who I am?

Des Lynam, Alan Hansen and Mark Lawrenson all die and go to Heaven, and find themselves standing before God at the pearly gates. God looks at them and says, 'Before granting you a place at my side, I must first ask you what you believe in.'

He asks Hansen, 'What do you believe?'

Al looks God in the eye and states passionately, 'I believe football to be the food of life. Nothing else brings such unbridled pleasure to so many people, from the slums of São Paulo, to the mansions of Chelsea. I have devoted my life to bringing joy to those people who stood on the terraces at Anfield.'

God looks up, and offers Alan the seat to his left. He then turns to Mark Lawrenson. 'And you, Mr Lawrenson. What do you believe?'

Mark stands tall and proud. 'I believe courage, honour and passion are the fundamentals of life, and I've spent my whole playing career providing a living embodiment of these traits.'

God, moved by the passion of this speech, offers Mark the seat to his right. Finally, he turns to Des Lynam. 'And you, Mr Lynam. What do you believe?'

'I believe', says Des smoothly, 'you are in my seat.'

Footballing flies

Some flies were playing football in a saucer, using a sugar lump as a ball. One of them said, 'We'll have to do better than this, lads. We're playing in the cup tomorrow.'

The memory man

A Brit was touring the USA on holiday and stopped in a remote bar in the hills of Nevada. He was chatting to the landlord when he spied an old Indian sitting in the corner. He wore tribal gear and had long white plaits and a wrinkled face.

'Who's he?' asked the Brit.

'That's the memory man,' said the landlord. 'He knows everything. He can remember any fact. Go and try him out.'

So the Brit went over and, thinking he won't know about English soccer, asked, 'Who won the 1965 FA Cup Final?'

'Liverpool,' replied the memory man.

'Who did they beat?'

'Leeds,' came the reply.

'And the score?'

'2–1.'

'Who scored the winning goal?'

'Ian St John' was the old man's reply. The Brit was knocked out by this and when he got back to the UK he told everyone there about the memory man.

A few years later, he went back to the USA and tried to find the impressive memory man. Eventually, he found the same bar and there, sitting in the same seat, was the old Indian. Only this time he was even older and more wrinkled.

Because he was so impressed, the Brit decided to greet the Indian in his native tongue. He approached him with the greeting, 'How.'

The memory man replied, 'Diving header in the six-yard box.'

Foot in mouth disease

'Barcelona ... a club with a stadium that seats 120,000 people. And they're all here in Newcastle tonight!'

'Ronaldo is always very close to being either onside or offside.'

'We were a little bit outnumbered there, it was two against two.'

'Julian Dicks is everywhere, it's like they've got 11 Dicks on the field.'

'If England are going to win this match, they're going to have to score a goal.'

'I never comment on referees and I'm not going to break the habit of a lifetime for that prat.'

'I'm not a believer in luck but I do believe you need it.'

'Celtic were at one time nine points ahead, but somewhere along the road, their ship went off the rails.'

'The new West Stand casts a giant shadow over the entire pitch, even on a sunny day.'

'I would not say he [David Ginola] is the best left-winger in the Premiership, but there are none better.'

'An inch or two either side of the post and that would have been a goal.'

'Both sides have scored a couple of goals, and both sides have conceded a couple of goals.'

'You don't score 64 goals in 86 games at the highest level without being able to score goals.'

'And we all know that in football if you stand still you go backwards ...'

'He had an eternity to play that ball, but he took too long over it.'

'The lad got over-excited when he saw the whites of the goal post's eyes.'

'He wasn't just facing one defender – he was facing one at the front and one at the back as well.'

'It's now 1–1, an exact reversal of the score on Saturday.'

'... but Arsenal are quick to credit Bergkamp with laying on 75% of their nine goals.'

'Gary always weighed up his options, especially when he had no choice.'

'We threw our dice into the ring and turned up trumps.'

'And I suppose they [Spurs] are nearer to being out of the FA Cup now than any other time since the first half of this season, when they weren't ever in it anyway.'

'If history is going to repeat itself I should think we can expect the same thing again.'

'Celtic manager Davie Hay still has a fresh pair of legs up his sleeve.'

'I spent four indifferent years at Goodison Park, but they were great years.'

'He's very fast and if he gets a yard ahead of himself nobody will catch him.'

'Nearly all the Brazilian players are wearing yellow shirts. It's a fabulous kaleidoscope of colour.'

'The game is balanced in Arsenal's favour.'

'Merseyside derbies usually last 90 minutes and I'm sure today's won't be any different.'

'Many clubs have a question mark in the shape of an axe-head hanging over them.'

'Dumbarton player Steve McCahill has limped off with a badly cut forehead.'

Top 10 reasons why football is better than sex ...

1 Balls are always checked for firmness.

2 Periods only last for 45 minutes.

3 Parents cheer when you score.

4 Soccer is a legal profession.

5 Protective equipment can be washed and reused.

6 Size doesn't matter.

7 If you get too rough you get a red card.

8 You can score using your head or your feet.

9 It lasts a full 90 minutes.

10 You can juggle your balls in front of your mother.

The Pope and Manchester United

A very holy young boy is going to the Vatican with his mum to see the Pope. The boy is a bit worried about whether or not they will see the Pope amongst the thousands of people. His mum says, 'Don't worry, son, the Pope is a big football fan, so I'll buy you a QPR strip. The Pope will see the famous hooped strip and he'll talk to you.'

So they buy the strip and the boy has it on while they are standing in the crowd as the Pope goes along in his Popemobile. Next thing, John Paul stops the Popemobile and gets out to talk to a different little boy wearing a Manchester United top. Then he gets back into the Popemobile and it drives right past the QPR fan. The little boy is very upset and is in tears.

'Don't worry,' says his mum. 'I'll buy you a Man. United strip, we'll come back tomorrow and then the Pope is guaranteed to stop and talk to you.'

So the boy comes back the next day, now wearing the Man. United shirt. The Popemobile comes along and the boy is all excited. The Popemobile stops and John Paul gets out, bends down to talk to the little boy, and says, 'I thought I told you to b****r off yesterday!'

Parachute fool

David Beckham, Thierry Henry, The Pope and a young schoolgirl are on a crashing plane and there are only three parachutes on board.

Henry says, 'I have to have one because I'm the star striker in the Premiership,' and out he jumps.

Beckham says, 'I have to have one because I'm England's best player,' and out he jumps.

The Pope says to the little girl, 'You have the last one as you have your whole life ahead of you.'

The little girl replies, 'No, we're both going to survive. David Beckham just jumped out with my school bag!'

Gone fishin'

Respect where it's due

Two men are sitting on a riverbank fishing. They look up at the bridge next to them and see a funeral procession passing over it.

One of the men stands up, takes his hat off and holds it over his heart, and bows.

The other man says, 'That was a very nice thing to do.'

The first man replies, 'Well, we were married for 25 years.'

Baited breath

A man went out to fish on a frozen lake. He cut a hole in the ice, dropped his line into the water beneath and sat for hours without so much as a nibble.

After a while, a boy came along and cut a hole nearby. He baited his line, dropped it into the hole and, within a few minutes, caught a fish. He baited his line again, and within another few minutes he had another fish. The man was incensed, so he went over to the boy and asked him his secret.

'Roo raf roo reep ra rums rrarm.'

'What was that?' the man asked.

Again the boy replied, 'Roo raf roo reep ra rums rrarm.'

'Look, I can't understand a word you're saying.'

The boy spat into his hand and said, 'You have to keep the worms warm.'

Where's the catch?

Two old guys were going on a fishing trip. They rented all the equipment: the reels, the rods, the wading suits, the boat, the car, and even a cabin in the woods. They spent a fortune.

On the first day's fishing they didn't catch anything. The same thing happened on the second day, and on the third day. It went on like this until, finally, on the last day of their holiday, one of the men caught a fish.

Driving home they felt really depressed. One bloke turned to the other and said, 'Do you realise that this one poxy fish we caught cost us a thousand pounds?' To which the other bloke replied, 'Wow! It's a good thing we didn't catch any more!'

Why fishing is better than sex

1 It's perfectly acceptable to pay a
   professional to fish with you once in
   a while.

2 You don't have to hide your fishing
   magazines.

3 The Ten Commandments don't say
   anything about fishing.

4 If your partner takes pictures or
   videotapes of you fishing in your boat,
   you don't have to worry about them
   showing up on the Internet if you
   become famous.

5 Your fishing partner doesn't get upset
   about people you fished with long ago.

6 It's perfectly respectable to fish with
   a total stranger.

7 When you see a really good fishing
   person, you don't have to feel guilty
   about imagining the two of you fishing
   in a boat together.

8 If your regular fishing partner isn't available, he/she won't object if you fish with someone else.

9 Nobody will ever tell you that you will go blind if you fish by yourself.

10 You can have a fishing calendar on your wall at the office, tell fishing jokes, and invite colleagues to fish with you without getting sued for harassment.

11 There are no fishing-transmitted diseases.

12 Your fishing partner will never say, 'Not again? We just fished together last week! Is fishing all you ever think about?'

Par for the course

Fore play

A golfer stood over his tee shot for what
seemed an eternity. He was driving his
partner mad as he looked up, looked down,
measured the distance, and worked out
the wind direction and speed. Finally, his
exasperated partner said, 'What's taking
so long? Hit the blasted ball!'

The bloke answered, 'My wife's up there watching me from the clubhouse. I want to make this a perfect shot.'

His partner mumbled, 'Forget it, man, you'll never hit her from here!'

A load of balls

A blonde golfer goes into the pro shop and looks around, frowning.

Finally the pro asks her what she wants. 'I can't find any green golf balls,' the blonde golfer complains.

The pro looks all over the shop, and through all the catalogues, and finally calls the manufacturers and determines that sure enough, there are no green golf balls.

As the blonde golfer walks out the door in disgust, the pro asks her, 'Before you go, could you tell me why you want green golf balls?'

'Well, obviously, because they would be so much easier to find in the bunkers!'

Nun unluckier

A nun sat with her Mother Superior chatting.

'I used some horrible language this week and feel absolutely terrible about it.'

'When did you use this awful language?' asked the elder.

'Well, I was golfing and hit an incredible drive that looked like it was going to make over 280 yards, but it struck a telegraph wire that was hanging over the fairway and fell straight down to the ground after going only about ten yards.'

'Is that when you swore?'

'No, Mother,' said the nun. 'After that, a squirrel ran out of the bushes and grabbed my ball in its mouth and began to run away.'

'Is THAT when you swore?' asked the Mother Superior again.

'Well, no,' said the nun. 'You see, as the squirrel was running along, an eagle came down out of the sky, grabbed the squirrel in his talons and began to fly away!'

'So, is THAT when you swore?' asked the amazed elder nun.

'No, not yet. As the eagle carried the squirrel away in its claws, it flew near the green and the squirrel dropped my ball.'

'Did you swear THEN?' asked the Mother Superior, becoming impatient.

'No, because the ball fell on a big rock, bounced over the bunker, rolled on to the green, and stopped about six inches from the hole.'

The two nuns were silent for a moment, then the Mother Superior sighed and said, 'You missed the f***ing putt, didn't you?'

One-track mind

A man is stranded on a desert island, all alone for ten years. One day, he sees a speck in the horizon. He thinks to himself, 'It's not a ship.' The speck gets a little closer and he thinks, 'It's not a boat.' The speck gets even closer and he thinks, 'It's not a raft.'

Then, out of the surf comes this gorgeous blonde woman, wearing a wetsuit and scuba-diving gear. She comes up to the bloke and says, 'How long has it been since you've had a cigarette?'

'Ten years!' he says.

She reaches over, unzips a waterproof pocket on her left sleeve and pulls out a pack of fresh cigarettes.

He takes one, lights it, takes a long drag, and says, 'Boy, oh boy! Is that good?!'

Then she asks, 'How long has it been since you've had a drink of whisky?'

He replies, 'Ten years!'

She reaches over, unzips the waterproof pocket on her right sleeve, pulls out a flask and gives it to him.

He takes a long swig and says, 'Wow, that's fantastic!'

Then she starts unzipping the longer zipper that runs down the front of her wetsuit and she says to him, 'And how long has it been since you've had some real fun?'

And the man replies, 'Wow! Don't tell me you've got golf clubs in there!'

Real blokes

Dos and don'ts for real blokes

1. Any man who takes a camera to a stag night may be legally killed and eaten by his fellow party-goers.

2. Under no circumstances may two men share an umbrella.

3. It is OK for a man to cry under the following circumstances:

a) when a heroic dog dies to save its master
b) the moment Angelina Jolie starts unbuttoning her blouse
c) after wrecking your boss's car
d) one hour, 12 minutes, 37 seconds into *The Crying Game*
e) when your date is using her teeth

4 Unless he murdered someone in your family, you must bail a friend out of jail within 12 hours.

5 Acceptable excuse for not helping a friend move house:

– your legs have been severed in a freak threshing accident.

6 Acceptable excuse for not helping a friend-of-a-friend move house:

– you'd rather stay home and watch last Saturday's Vauxhall Conference League highlights.

7 If you've known a bloke for more than 24 hours, his sister is off-limits forever, unless you actually marry her.

8 The minimum amount of time you have to wait for a bloke who's running late is five minutes. The maximum waiting time is six minutes. For a girl, you have to wait ten minutes for every 'point of hotness' she scores on the classic 1–10 scale.

9 Moaning about the brand of free beer in a mate's fridge is forbidden. Gripe at will if the temperature is unsuitable.

10 No man shall ever be required to buy a birthday present for another man (in fact, even remembering your mate's birthday is strictly optional).

11 On a long drive, the strongest bladder determines pit-stops, not the weakest.

12 While your girlfriend must bond with your mates' girlfriends within 30 minutes of meeting them, you are not required to get on with her girlfriends' significant others; low-level sports bonding is all the law requires.

13 When stumbling upon other guys watching a sporting event, you may always ask the score of the game in progress, but you may never ask who's playing.

14 It is permissible to quaff a fruity girly drink only when you are sunning yourself on a tropical beach ... and a topless supermodel delivers it ... and it's free.

15 Only in situations of moral and/or mortal peril are you allowed to kick another bloke in the nuts.

16 Unless you're in prison, never fight naked.

17 If a man's flies are open, that's his problem – you didn't see anything.

18 Women who claim they 'love to watch football' must be treated as spies until they demonstrate knowledge of the game and the ability to drink as much beer as their fellow football-watchers.

19 If you compliment a bloke on his six-pack, you'd better be talking about his choice of lager.

20 Phrases that may not be uttered to another man while lifting weights:
a) Yeah, baby! Push it!
b) C'mon, give me one more! Harder!
c) Another set and we can hit the showers!
d) Nice arse, are you a Sagittarius?

21 Never compliment a man you have never met on his tan in the shower.

22 Never talk to a man in the gents unless you are on an equal footing: both urinating, both waiting in line, etc. For all other situations, an almost imperceptible nod is all the conversation you need.

23 You may fart in front of a woman only after you have brought her to climax. If you trap her head under the covers for the purpose of flatulent entertainment, she is officially your girlfriend.

First published in the UK in 2003 exclusively for
WHSmith
Greenbridge Road
Swindon SN3 3LD
www.WHSmith.co.uk

by The Orion Publishing Group
5 Upper St Martin's Lane
London
WC2H 9EA

A CIP record for this book is available from the British Library

Design and typesetting by SMPS Ltd, Haverhill, Suffolk
Illustrations by Bill Ledger

ISBN 1898799571

Printed in Italy